Katharina von Bora

Hero of Faith

By Jane L. Fryar

Illustrated by Deborah J. White

CONCORDIA PUBLISHING HOUSE · SAINT LOUIS

Copyright © 2011 Concordia Publishing House
3558 S. Jefferson Ave., St. Louis, MO 63118-3968
1-800-325-3040 · www.cph.org

Written by Jane L. Fryar
Illustrated by Deborah J. White
Edited by Rodney L. Rathmann
Editorial assistant: Amanda G. Lansche

Manufactured in Green Bay, WI /055101/416354

Table of Contents

Katie said good-bye and they were off.

chapter one

Changed Forever

Katie felt hot tears well up in her eyes as her father's horses trotted down the bumpy dirt road, taking her farther from home than she had ever been before. Sitting in the wagon next to Papa, she had always felt safe. Leaving the von Bora family estate near Hirschfeld had always been an adventure. Not today.

Today, Katie had said good-bye to her brothers, her stepmother, and her stepbrothers. Today, Katie had heard her family's big wooden front door close tight behind her for the last time. The wagon creaked as Papa hoisted six-year-old Katharina von Bora up into her seat. It creaked again as he had come around to the other side of the wagon and clambered up to sit beside her. He flicked the reins, and they were off.

It was late summer. The wagon lumbered past the garden where Katie had helped to plant cabbages and pull weeds. It took Katie past the village church where she had been baptized, its whitewashed walls gleaming in the morning sun.

Later in her life, people would call Katie tough and persistent. She had to be. Her mother, Anna von Haugwitz, died when Katie was five. Her papa, Hans von Bora, struggled to keep his little family going. But before long, he knew he must marry again—both for the sake of his children and because he needed help farming the family estate.

That's why, only a few months after her mother's death, Katie found herself welcoming her stepmother, Margarete von Seidewitz, into the von Bora home. And it's why six-year-old Katie sat in Papa's wagon that day in 1505, headed for the convent school that would be her new home.

The once-proud von Bora family had fallen on hard times. They weren't the only ones. The late 1400s and early 1500s brought many tumultuous changes all over Europe. The feudal system with its knights and lords, its manor houses and nobility, was ending. A merchant class, funded by bankers and spurred on by explorers, was rising in its place.

Her mother, Anna von Haugwitz,
died when Katie was five.

Christopher Columbus had "sailed the ocean blue" for the first time in 1492—seven years before Katie's birth on January 29, 1499. His voyages had encouraged others to set off in search of fame and fortune. Before this time, people bartered for what they needed. Now, more and more, they were using money instead of trading goods and services.

Katie's ancestors would not have recognized this new world. Gone were the serfs—the bond servants who once helped farm the von Bora property. Gone was the glory of that estate. Once upon a time, the "von" in Hans von Bora's name had reminded the world of the family's noble, knightly bloodline. Now, it reminded Katie's papa of how far the family's fortunes had fallen.

Still, they had their land. It was one of the few things people could count on. If you had land, you could grow food. Land and the buildings on it provided shelter. And owning land meant social status.

On the other hand, it took hard work to eke out a living from the earth. Even very young children worked right beside their parents in garden and field. Strong sons were a special blessing. When fathers died, sons inherited the family's land.

Daughters, though, were usually another story. Teenage daughters got married. But love, as we think of it today, meant little. Instead, parents chose likely husbands for their daughters. They paid the new husband's family a dowry—land, livestock, or money. In general, the bigger the dowry, the better the family into which the daughter could marry. And the easier the new wife's life could be.

Hans von Bora saw he had little hope of providing a proper dowry for Katie. And so, it seems, he chose for Katie the second life path open to girls in that day. He would see to it that she received an education. Then he would send her to a convent to live out her life. With the other nuns, she would pray. Perhaps she would care for sick people. Maybe she would teach.

Hans could not see into Katie's future, but he knew he could place his daughter into God's hands. There, she would be safe despite the changes and challenges swallowing up the old world.

Maybe Hans von Bora thought about all this as he flicked the reins, urging his horses on. Or maybe not. Either way, the changes and challenges swirling through society were about to change Katie's life forever.

◆ ◆ ◆

chapter two

Right-side Up, Upside Down

Hans von Bora's wagon rumbled to a halt outside the gates of the Benedictine abbey at Brehna. As Papa lifted Katie down from her seat on the wagon, she felt stiff and a bit sore. She stood up and down on her tiptoes to stretch her legs. The trip had taken two days.

Katie had seen more in those two days than ever before in her life. The wagon had bounced along through fertile meadowlands. It had passed cropland and pastures. Katie had peered deep into the water of the Mulde River as Papa's horses trotted across the bridge there. Then came Leipzig—a city bigger than any Katie could have imagined! Later, as the horses trotted past Delitzsch, Papa pointed out the weaving mills that had sprung up there.

Arriving at the Benedictine abbey: the trip had taken two days.

For a time, the wonder of all these new sights had kept Katie's mind busy. But now, finally at the convent and standing beside Papa's two big workhorses, Katie felt the butterflies in her stomach flying faster. She craned her neck toward the sky, looking up as far as she could see. The cross atop the tall steeple of the church at Brehna seemed to touch the clouds. The church sat at the very center of the convent. And it would stand at the center of Katie's life for the next four years too.

It didn't take long for Papa to finish his conversation with the head of the convent and to pay the fee that made it possible for Katie to stay. He bent down to give his little daughter a quick kiss. Then, lifting himself into the wagon, he snapped the reins and turned back toward Hirschfeld. He was gone in a moment. As he left, he took with him most of what Katie found familiar and comforting. It must have seemed in that moment as though her entire world lurched and turned upside down.

The cross atop the tall steeple of the church at Brehna seemed to touch the clouds.

Mercifully, Katie had little time to think about her loneliness. The school at Brehna had a good reputation. Girls sent there studied hard. They learned to read and write. They learned the Lord's Prayer. They learned to sing the psalms. They learned all about church symbols and the liturgy. In addition, they learned how being members of noble families affected their faith and their actions.

Katie did not spend all her time in school, though. A number of important buildings ringed the cloister church. These hint at what the rest of Katie's life at Brehna must have been like.

For instance, she would have eaten her meals in the refectory, a building with a large open room and long, wooden tables. All the girls, their teachers, and the other nuns who lived at the convent would have eaten together there.

There was also a bakery and a kitchen. Perhaps Katie learned to make bread. Perhaps she chopped up vegetables or even made apple dumplings. There were cellars nearby—cool underground storage areas for root crops, apples, and wine.

A refectory was a building with a large open room and long, wooden tables.

Beyond this circle of buildings stood yet another. This ring included the schoolhouse where Katie studied and the building in which she and all the other students lived. The infirmary stood nearby too. Perhaps Katie and the other girls helped there when sick or injured people from the town of Brehna or the nearby villages came to the convent for treatment.

Farther out lay barns for livestock and shops for craftsmen and artists. Maybe Katie and her friends sneaked out to catch a glimpse of baby pigs in spring. Maybe they watched the artisans paint portraits or create stained glass or sculpt statues of the saints.

Life at Brehna was busy. But just as the cloister church lay in the center of the abbey, so worship lay at the center of everyone's attention. In most convents and monasteries of that time, the nuns and monks gathered for prayer seven times a day. No one knows if the convent at Brehna required the students who stayed there to attend all seven of these daily services. But no doubt, Katie and her friends worshiped many times a day, every day of the week.

Here, in worship, Katie touched the familiar. Here, she heard some of the music she remembered from her little church at home in Hirschfeld. Here, week by week, she heard the familiar words of the liturgy. Now, as she learned Latin, she could begin to understand some of those words. (All worship services in Europe at that time were conducted in Latin.) Here, she prayed the Our Father and some of the other prayers she had learned at home from her mother when she was very young. All these familiar things must have comforted her.

Katie sang the psalms. She studied her Latin. She confessed her sins to the priests. She harvested kohlrabi and carried it to the root cellar. She ate thick soup and bread pudding. She giggled with her friends at the newborn calf trying to stand on its own four feet for the first time. She adjusted to life at Brehna. Little by little, life turned right-side up.

But before long, changes would turn Katie's life upside down once again.

chapter three

Into the Convent

Sister Katharina sat straight up in bed, startled. As she tried to remember where she was, she realized the bell for Matins had awakened her. It was 1:00 a.m. Quickly, she forced her feet onto the cold floorboards. She made the sign of the cross over her heart and slipped on her white habit. Then, a second bell rang. She opened the door of her cell and moved with the other nuns in the convent down the corridor and toward the simple church.

The "white sisters," so named for the color of their habits, prayed many times each twenty-four-hour period. After Matins came a service known as Lauds. Each service lasted about an hour. At about 3:00 a.m., everyone would go back to bed until 6:00 a.m. Five more services punctuated the day. Finally, at 8:00 p.m. came Compline—the last service before bedtime.

Most orders of nuns and monks at this time followed a similar schedule for prayer. They considered prayer their main work. Each order, or group, of monks and nuns followed a different rule, or way of life. These rules were alike in many ways, but they were different in some ways too.

Most rules were very strict. In fact, the orders sometimes competed with each other to see who could serve God more by living the hardest lives—they mistakenly believed that suffering earned His favor. Nuns lived in convents and were called "sisters." Monks lived in monasteries and were known as "brothers." Priests served both groups and were called "fathers." Some orders had both convents and monasteries; other orders included only sisters or only brothers.

By the time Katie von Bora entered the Benedictine convent in Brehna, the Benedictine order had been in existence for centuries. Like other orders, the Benedictines helped the poor, sick, and travelers. Some orders focused more on teaching, others focused on other work. But by 1500, all the orders in the church concentrated on one main thing: adding up good deeds for themselves and for others outside their order.

They did this because they saw God as an angry judge. By their good deeds, they hoped to escape punishment and hell. They also did it to shorten the time they, their family members, and others, would spend in purgatory.

Benedictines helped the poor, sick, and travelers.

The church taught that purgatory was a place that stood between earth and heaven. In purgatory, Christians supposedly suffered for their "minor" sins committed on earth. (The Bible says nothing about a place between earth and heaven. In fact, Hebrews 9:27 teaches, "It is appointed for man to die once, and after that comes judgment.")

Praying. Fasting. Taking vows of silence. Giving away all of one's possessions. Living in poverty. Refusing to marry. Obeying the person in charge of the order. All these were ways to please God and make up for one's sins. Some monks and nuns were so worried about their sins, they even hurt themselves. For example, they would beat themselves bloody to punish themselves for their sins.

Some monks and nuns beat themselves as punishment for their sins.

Katie's first convent followed the rule of St. Benedict. She spent about four years there. After Katie's schooling was finished, Hans von Bora had paid a second fee to another convent run by the Cistercian sisters. It was in Nimbschen. The fee was much lower than it would have been if Hans had enrolled Katie at Brehna's convent. Perhaps that is why he chose it. Katie's first days and weeks in Nimbschen must have been quite difficult.

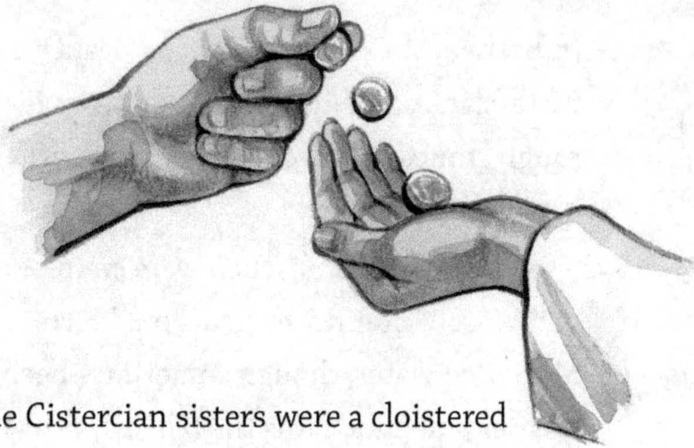

The Cistercian sisters were a cloistered order. This meant outside visitors were forbidden. Two guards even stood at the gates to enforce this rule. The Cistercian sisters followed the Benedictine rule, but much more strictly than the sisters at Brehna. For example, the Cistercian sisters never spoke. They used their voices only to sing the liturgy. One sister was chosen each day to read aloud from the rules of their order during meals. Otherwise, everyone used a kind of sign language members of the order had made up over the years.

The buildings were much rougher and not nearly as architecturally pleasing as those at the convent in Brehna. All glass was clear—no stained glass here. The only art Katharina and the other nuns could display in their small rooms, or cells, would have been a simple crucifix or a relief of the Virgin Mary.

In Brehna, the church had been beautiful. The Cistercians worshiped in a building made of rough stones that looked like all the other buildings in the complex.

Meals at Nimbschen were simple too. For breakfast, Sister Katharina would have eaten bread and water, though sometimes beer or wine was served. Lunch was the biggest meal of the day. The sisters ate vegetables, raisins, almonds, figs, and some kind of meat, most of it grown right on the convent grounds. On Friday, they would have enjoyed fish from the large convent pond or herring (a kind of salted fish) purchased from Leonhard Koppe, a merchant from the nearby town of Torgau. Supper consisted of a simple soup, bread, and beverages.

Katie learned many skills at the convent.

As far as Hans von Bora knew, his little Katie would live out her days among the Cistercians. She got along well there. After her postulate—a kind of trial period that lasted several years—she took her vows in 1515. She was sixteen. As Sister Katharina, she would be "married to Christ" forever rather than marrying a man and starting a family.

She threw herself into her work. She learned many skills, including how to apply many herbal treatments to bring healing. She prayed fervently. She obeyed the abbess in charge.

Even in the silence of the cloister, though, news from the outside world was leaking in. Little by little, the hearts of several Cistercian nuns were coming to see God in new and freeing ways. Sister Katharina was among them.

chapter four

Freedom!

Sister Margarete dipped her quill into the ink and began to write. "To the highly learned Dr. Martinus Luther at Wittenberg," the letter began. Eleven other nuns crowded around her in the darkened schoolroom, whispering quietly. They could not let themselves be overheard.

For months now, they had been reading Dr. Martin Luther's writings. Someone had smuggled these forbidden materials into the convent. No one knows for sure, but the herring merchant, Leonhard Koppe, is a likely suspect. He was one of only very few people from outside the convent who had contact with the cloistered nuns of Nimbschen. And he was a friend and supporter of Luther.

Luther—once a monk himself, belonging to the Augustinian order—had written forcefully about the abuses suffered by monks and, especially, nuns. He had also written about the freedom of the Christian. He stressed the grace of God. He asserted that Jesus' death on the cross paid the price for every sin; nothing we can do will make our heavenly Father love us more. Faith receives this Good News and lives in joy and peace. Christians do good works, not to earn forgiveness, but because we know we are already forgiven!

We can't imagine how this great news—the Gospel—must have stirred the hearts of the nuns of Nimbschen. After much prayer and thought, many of them secretly wrote their families, asking permission to come home. They waited and waited, but there was no response.

Martin Luther proclaimed that Jesus died on the cross to pay the price for every sin!

Twelve nuns put together a bold plan.

Some, like Sister Katharina, could not contact their families. These family estates lay in the hands of Roman Catholic rulers. Helping a nun or monk escape carried the death penalty! At the very least, the family would lose its status. Making a living would be very difficult. And taking a grown daughter back would mean another mouth to feed at a time when most families were very poor.

Finally, the twelve nuns could wait no longer. They put together a bold plan. They would contact Luther himself. The leader of the Reformation would have to help them, they thought, especially after all he had written about freedom! They poured out their hearts in a letter to him.

This letter these sisters composed must have come as some surprise to Luther. Only a few years earlier, Pope Leo X had excommunicated him. It had sealed his break with the Roman Catholic Church. It had also put his life in grave danger—so much so that his prince and friend, Elector Frederick, had secretly kidnapped him. Luther spent nearly a year secluded in Wartburg Castle under his friend's protection. Luther had eventually left the castle, but his life was still in danger.

Now, twelve nuns were seeking his help. Surely, Luther thought and prayed, prayed and thought. Finally, he acted. He called on his friend and supporter Leonhard Koppe for help. Somehow, Koppe got word to the sisters. The escape was set for very early on Easter Day, 1523.

Koppe enlisted two friends. As quietly as possible, they drove Koppe's freight wagon through the darkness toward the convent. While everyone else slept, the twelve sisters slipped outside. When Koppe arrived, he and his friends helped Katharina and the others into the back of the wagon, which held some herring barrels. There, they hid in the dark. Then Koppe and the other two men lifted themselves into the driver's seat. Koppe flicked the reins. They were off.

The nuns brought with them only the white habits they wore and perhaps a shawl to warm themselves against the cold April air. The wagon planks were hard, and there were likely no blankets to soften the bumps and jolts.

Worse than the physical discomfort, though, was the anxiety. Would someone come after them? Were their lives in danger? Surely, thoughts like these must have raced through the minds of Katharina and her friends. They prayed earnestly for God's protection.

But once they passed the dark forest of Grimma, they were safe. Their convent had no mounted guards who could come after them. Still, Koppe chose back, country roads and stayed out of territory ruled by Roman Catholic princes.

Then, in the distance, church bells began to announce the dawn of Easter Day. "Christ is risen!" the bells proclaimed. "Christ is risen! And we are free!" Katharina and her friends must have said to one another.

Katharina's world had just turned upside down—yet again! This time, in a wonderful way. But now a new set of problems confronted each of them. How would they live? How would they feed and clothe themselves? Where would they find shelter? Who would protect them? These were very real and very serious questions for single women in sixteenth century Europe.

Later, as Katharina reflected back on these days, she would see her heavenly Father's protecting care. It was unmistakable. The Lord whom she had loved and served would not let her down. He loved her even more than she could imagine. And He would provide for her in wonderful ways. Still, as the wagon lurched along through the cold April sunshine, all that lay ahead, shrouded in uncertainty.

"Christ is risen! And we are free!"

"Hurry!" begged Katie.

chapter five

"My Lord Katie"

The locksmith strode into Lutherhaus with his tools. "Hurry!" begged Katie, leading him up the winding staircase to the third floor. Martin Luther had closed the big wooden door of his study behind himself three days before. He was writing again.

Throughout their marriage, Katie did all she could to make sure Martin had peace and quiet for his writing. He considered it one of the most important parts of his work. This time, Dr. Luther was focused on Psalm 22—the psalm that so powerfully describes Jesus' death and His resurrection victory. This message lay at the very heart of the Gospel, and Luther was thrilled at the opportunity to interpret this psalm so other Christians could grow in faith.

But Martin had taken only a little bread, salt, and water to his study with him. Despite Katie's knocking, pleas, and shouts, he had not answered. Now, she was afraid he had fallen ill or perhaps even died!

The locksmith took out a sturdy hammer and began banging away, taking the heavy door off its hinges. Moments later, he picked it up in his brawny arms and moved it aside.

There at his desk sat Dr. Luther, quill pen in hand. He blinked and frowned in surprise. Katie sighed in relief. Then, as the locksmith began to reattach the door, she began to scold. When she paused to take a breath, Martin asked Katie, "Do you think I was up to something bad?"

This incident reveals a lot about their marriage. He focused intently on his work; she protected and cared for him. He was often unaware of anything but his work; she, often exasperated, was always deeply concerned for his welfare.

"Do you think I was up to something bad?"

Katharina von Bora and Martin Luther marry in 1525.

Martin had never intended to marry, least of all any of the nuns Leonhard Koppe had freed from the convent at Nimbschen. But he did feel responsible for them. After a few weeks, some had gone home to their families. The people of Wittenberg had found husbands for others. Luther's friends had proposed to one or two. Finally, almost two years after the rescue mission, only Katharina von Bora remained in Wittenberg, alone and unmarried. She was twenty-six—well past the age most people at that time considered marriageable.

Finally, in 1525, Luther proposed. Katharina accepted. They moved into the Black Cloister in Wittenberg, where Luther had been living. It was like a big, drafty hotel or hospital. At one time, as many as forty Augustinian monks had made their home there. In fact, the cloister had gotten its name from the color of the robes worn by those monks. Now, one by one, the monks had moved all out, freed—as Katie had been—by the Good News of salvation by Christ alone, through faith alone. Everyone, that is, except Martin himself.

Katharina must have shaken her head at the disarray she found the first time she walked through the front door. Dr. Luther's work absorbed him. He often traveled. His responsibilities left him little time to take care of the property. On their wedding day, Katie found that Martin had not changed the straw in his bed for over a year! (Imagine the bugs and even mice that must have been living in it!)

Katie set to work. She whitewashed walls. She planted gardens. She bought livestock. She bred riding horses. She brewed beer. She welcomed dozens of guests to Lutherhaus (Luther House) and fed them. Before long, she was managing a staff of many workers, all hired to help. Martin had little interest in the family budget or in running the household. He turned it all over to Katie.

Katie welcomed many guests to Lutherhaus.

Before long, the Luthers' first son, Hans, was born (1526). Five more children followed: Elizabeth in 1527, Magdalene in 1529, Martin in 1531, Paul in 1533, and Margarete in 1534. The Luthers also raised four orphaned children, including one of Katie's nephews.

Sadly, Elizabeth died just eight months after her birth. Sadder still, Magdalene died in 1542, at age 13. These two losses nearly broke Martin's and Katie's hearts. Only their hope in Christ and in His resurrection sustained them. Martin wrote, "This is my reason for joy—that [Magdalene] lives. In the arms of her true Father, she sleeps until the day of her resurrection."

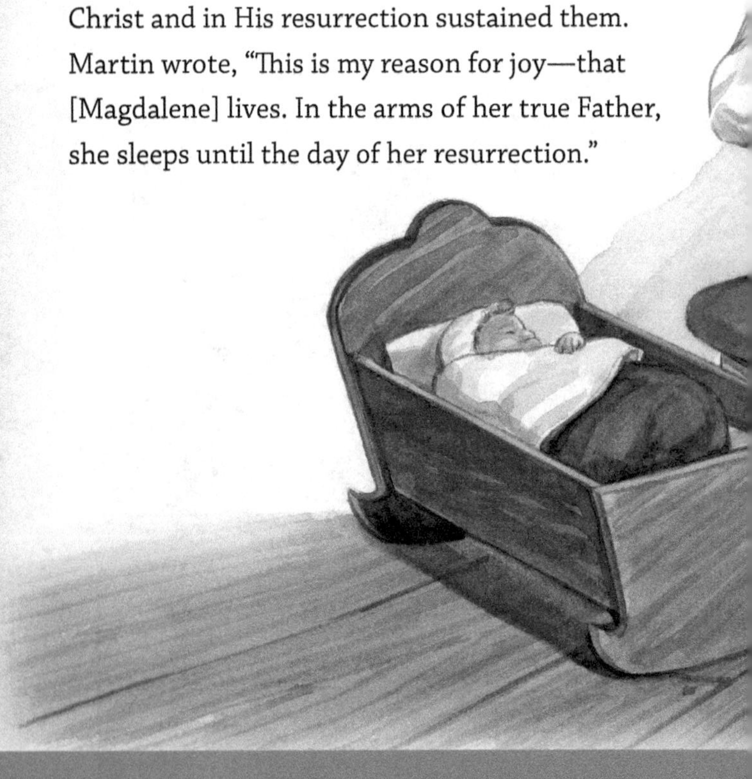

Little by little, through all the trials and blessings of life together, Martin and Katie came to respect and love each other more and more. When they had first met, Martin considered Katie stubborn and proud. Soon, though, he came to admire her strength. When he was away from home, he often wrote to her, calling her at various times "Lord Katharina," "Doctor and Professor," and "the Lady of the Pig Market." In this last title,

Martin was teasing Katie for having purchased a garden on the outskirts of Wittenberg. The garden lay next to the place where live pigs were sold.

When Martin was at home, students and friends often gathered at Lutherhaus to discuss theology. Martin included Katie in these discussions. Some of the men at these "table talk" events thought her presence improper. But Martin ignored their objections, valuing her contributions.

Music and theology. Children's games and travel plans. Flowers and vegetables from the garden. New foals in the barn and sick people for Katie to nurse in the guest rooms. Life at Lutherhaus bustled. Martin and his work flourished under Katie's watchful, courageous care.

Theological discussions were held at the Luther table.

chapter six

The Morning Star of the Reformation

Once again, Katie found herself bumping along in a wagon that was taking her away from home. The year was 1552. Her beloved Martin had died in 1546, six years earlier. While he had loved her with all his heart, he had not created a plan for her and their children in the event of his death.

Martin's death had nearly crushed Katie. Besides the grief, it also brought serious financial hardship. Martin's salary as a professor and pastor ended the day he died. In that time, no church pensions or government programs protected widows—not even pastors' widows—from poverty.

In addition, two wars swept quickly, one by one, across the region. These put Katie and her children in grave danger. Each time, Katie packed up a few belongings and fled from Wittenberg to safer places. Each time she returned home, she found Lutherhaus, the home and gardens she and Martin had shared, damaged and in more desperate need of repair.

A few influential friends—the Elector John Frederick, King Christian III of Denmark, and others—helped Katie and her family a little, providing some funds to meet their financial needs. But this was not until after Katie had written several letters, almost begging for help.

Now, Katie was fleeing Wittenberg for the third time, but not because of war. This time, she fled because the Black Plague had overtaken the city. Paul and Margarete, both now in their late teens, went with her. They would all be safer in Torgau.

Black Plague devastates the region, causing Katie and her children to flee.

As their cart jolted along through the crisp morning air, perhaps Katie remembered another morning about fifty years earlier. Perhaps she closed her eyes and imagined sitting beside Papa on the driver's seat of their family wagon behind the big workhorses. Perhaps she thought back to the convent school in Brehna, remembering Jesus' care for her as she studied her Latin. Perhaps she repeated the words of one of the psalms she had sung as a little girl in the convent church.

Or maybe she remembered Leonhard Koppe's wagon. Perhaps she thought back to those herring barrels, to her white habit, to the sun breaking over the horizon, and to the church bells ringing. Perhaps she thought about how she and her eleven sisters in the faith hid with those barrels that early Easter morning.

Perhaps she said to herself,

"Christ is risen!"

Maybe she even added,

"And we are free!"

Katie remembers.

Suddenly, the horses pulling Katie's cart saw something that frightened them. They shied. The cart lurched wildly. Worried for her children, Katie jumped down to try to calm the horses. She hit the ground—hard. It knocked the breath from her lungs. She rolled into a ditch filled with water. It was November, and the water was freezing cold.

Katie hit the ground hard.

Beside themselves with fear for their mother, Paul and Margarete both jumped down to help. They calmed the horses and helped Katie into the back of the cart. Then they headed toward their destination, the city of Torgau, once again.

Along the way and after they arrived, their mother's condition grew worse. For three months, Katharina hung between life and death. The fall. The shock. The cold and exposure. Perhaps internal injuries. All these combined proved to be too much. On December 20, 1552, Katharina von Bora Luther went to meet the Savior she had loved, worshiped, and served all her life. She was fifty-three.

Katharina died on December 20, 1552. She was fifty-three.

Often when people die, those left behind think about the question of legacy. What did the person leave behind? What difference did his or her life make?

Katie left a wonderful legacy, one worked by the Holy Spirit in Katie's heart and life.

Though she would be the first to accuse herself of weakness of faith and failure in prayer, Katie lived a life of faith and prayer that truly honored Jesus. Looking back at her courageous decisions and strong character, we thank Him.

And we see proof that the Lord defends His faithful people. He hears and answers our prayers.

Only God knows how Martin Luther's ministry would have been different had he not had Katie as his wife. Without her care, the great reformer's life might have been much shorter. He surely would not have written as much. He would not have been as able to tie his sermons and books so closely to real life in real families. The Holy Spirit used Katie and Martin's talks and prayers to shape the faith they shared.

Katie's example as a wife, mother, household manager, and child of God changed the ways people thought about women, about families, and about children. It helped people see that one's vocation (or calling) from God need not mean living in a cloister. Taking care of a home, helping children grow up as Christians, sharing the joys and challenges of family life—these, too, could be God's calling. This work pleases the Savior just as much as or maybe even more than life behind convent walls.

Martin had once called Katie "the Morning Star of the Reformation" because she usually got up at 4:30 to begin her work at Lutherhaus.

Given his respect and love for her, he may have meant much more by that name. Just as the morning star shines brightly in the eastern sky before dawn, Katharina's life shone brightly with the love Jesus had shown her.

That same Savior lives in you too! Just as He called Katie in her Baptism to serve Him by serving others, He is calling you! What shape will your service take?

Timeline of Events

during Katharina von Bora's Life

1499 Katharina's birth (January 29)

1503 Leonardo da Vinci begins painting the Mona Lisa

1505 Katharina's mother dies; Katharina, age six, enters convent school at Brehna

1506 Christopher Columbus dies

1507 Martin Luther ordained as a priest

1508 Michelangelo begins painting Sistine Chapel

1509 Hans von Bora moves Katharina, age ten, to the Cistercian convent at Nimbschen

1512 Martin Luther receives doctoral degree in theology, begins teaching in Wittenberg

1513 Ponce de Leon discovers Florida; Balboa sees the Pacific Ocean

1515 Sister Katharina, age sixteen, takes vows

1517 Martin Luther posts the Ninety-five Theses on Wittenberg's church door

1518 Officials in Rome begin a formal inquiry about Luther's teachings

1519 Magellan begins voyage to circumnavigate the globe

1520 Luther burns the pope's papal bull

1521 Luther excommunicated from the Roman Catholic Church; Luther ordered to Worms to stand trial for heresy; death sentence imposed; Luther is kidnapped by friends and hidden in the castle at Wartburg

1522 Luther returns to Wittenberg

1523 Sister Katharina and eleven other sisters write Dr. Martin Luther to ask for his help in escaping

1525 Katharina marries Martin Luther; Katharina is twenty-six, Martin is forty-two; they make their home in Wittenberg

1526 The Luthers' first son, Hans, is born

1527 The Luthers' first daughter, Elizabeth, is born; she dies eight months later in 1528

1529 Daughter Magdalene is born

1531 Son Martin is born and named after his father

1533 Son Paul is born and named after the apostle whose writings brought both his parents such comfort

1534 Luther publishes full translation of German Old and New Testaments; Daughter Margarete is born; Henry VIII breaks with Rome, establishing the Church of England

1539 Katharina suffers a miscarriage

1542 Magdalene dies at age thirteen

1543 Copernicus publishes document announcing sun as center of universe

1546 Dr. Luther dies; Katharina is forced to flee with her children to Magdeburg when the Smalkaldian War breaks out

1547 Katharina returns to Wittenberg to find destruction and endure poverty

1549 Christianity reaches Japan

1552 Plague and crop failure force Katharina to flee to Torgau; she's injured on the way and dies three months later (December 20) at age fifty-three